T0150784

# Love is
# Freedom

# Love is Freedom

## Joseph Murphy
### Ph.D., D.D.

MEDIA

MEDIA

Published 2019 by Gildan Media LLC
aka G&D Media
www.GandDmedia.com

Design by Meghan Day Healey of Story Horse, LLC

Library of Congress Cataloging-in-Publication Data is available upon request

ISBN: 978-1-7225-0131-0

10   9   8   7   6   5   4   3   2   1

*Dedicated to Vere Brunt*
*who suggested the title of this book.*

# Contents

# Contents

# Foreword

True mysticism is the ability inwardly to sense the invisible things of Spirit and through feeling, present them to the intellect.

In discerning the deep things of the Spirit, the intellect must follow the intuition—and it will never follow it in vain, for that which the intuition reveals, the intellect may later analyze. It is this feeling back toward spiritual prototypes that marks the work of the true mystic in any age.

In this book Joseph Murphy, one of the outstanding mystics in the metaphysical field, has presented a depth of feeling seldom expressed through the written word.

Those who have had the privilege of listening to the discourses of Dr. Murphy have felt that which was not spoken, the impartation of a spiritual essence which can only be felt. I am certain that the readers of this book will find a response in their consciousness to that invisible and ineffable beauty which it suggests.

*Ernest Holmes*
*President and Founder of Institute of*
*Religious Science and Philosophy,*
*Los Angeles, California*

# Introduction

## by Joseph Murphy

The Bible has been said to have seven layers of meaning:

1. The physical and historical. All Scripture was held (by ORIGEN) to be written "ab intus," from the inward mystery, and not "ab extra" with a mystical sense *put into it. In every case* the historical account is the rind or coating, the mystical meaning being the essence of Holy Scripture— not the former *the* essential truth containing a mystical sense. As St. Paul says (I Cor. 2:14), the truth of the Scriptures must be 'spiritually discerned'. This implies that the inspired element is underneath the phraseology rather than on it. We must drill beyond the merely semantic layers

and sands before "the oil" of the Spirit "is struck" and "a gusher" is brought in.

2. The solar—dealing with the garden in which man finds himself.

3. The phallic—concerning the throb of life coursing through all animate beings.

4. The mental—which is ruler over many things, but not all.

5. The psychic—which approaches the Holy of Holies, but does not always "make it" because of astral distractions in the forest of illusion. (Hindu Maya)

6. The mystic—in which the seeker longs for God as "the heart panteth after the water brooks". Many falter on the way here as they get stuck in the mire of the mere play of mental operations, which practice often misses the "manna" falling from the Throne of God. (I and the Father are one type of consciousness.)

7. The absolute spiritual consciousness in which God functions through the God-man outlet.

We must remember that there are many overtones in the field of consciousness. "There are many mansions in my Father's House." There is an atomic science of the spirit also, with its own wavelengths and electronics. Let us enter into the high oscillations of the spirit by focusing our attention on "He who Is". "If thine eye be single, thy whole body is full of light." "With mine eyes stayed on Thee, there is no evil in my pathway." This viewpoint requires skillful "mountain" climbing with the mystics' sure-footedness like "hinds' feet" and not mere elementary psychology or hypnotics. We must seek reality "In Him whom to know aright" is the highest wisdom. For God is—He was not made.

# Chapter 1

The scripture says, "God is love, God is all, over all, through all, all in all." Therefore, love is resident in all men and in all things. And so let us seek it in all. "Seek and ye shall find." Yes, if you truly look for the God love in the other it will shine forth in all its pristine glory. The first thing we do when we see another is to look for that Divine Love to radiate through his thoughts, words and deeds. If we truly recognize it as being within him, it must certainly appear on the without. "As within, so without." "As above so below." "As in heaven (consciousness) so on earth (manifestation)."

We must not let fear step in—for it is the opposite of love. There is only Love, and fear is the inversion of Love, or Love turned upside down. If man recognizes Love in a dog, the animal responds in kind. When we fear the dog or any other animal, the latter senses it and it strikes up a similar response in him.

When we are faced with a problem let us become still and feel within ourselves that the Divine Love is working through the situation now and that only harmony and peace prevail, and then dismiss it from our minds knowing that it is so. We will find a perfect solution is offered us which blesses all.

A woman told me a few years ago that her son was an aviator during the war. Each night while he was away, all she did was simply to take her son in her arms in meditation, realizing that Divine Love enfolded him in the midst of the chaos of war. The aura of His Love surrounded the plane, always making it invisible to the so-called enemy. The boy was never attacked; the enemy planes never "saw" him, so how could they attack him.

Jesus disappeared in the multitude. Yes, the multitude of human thoughts and false beliefs disappear when the shining armor of Truth comes rushing in, lighting up the whole house. Then the dawn appears and the shadows vanish.

# Chapter 2

≫⧫ · · · · · · · · ⧫≪

*"Though I speak with the tongues of men and of angels, and have not charity, I am become as sounding brass, or a tinkling cymbal."*

—(I Cor. 13:1)

This is the greatest Love Epic ever written. If men and women were to meditate on the inner meaning of this chapter, one of the greatest in the Bible, their lives would be transformed. It is only too true that men use high-sounding words, write beautiful poetry and give wonderful sermons, yet unless these words be permeated with love and feeling they are empty.

For example, a man told me recently that his mother was dying in the hospital. His sister visited him, and together they went to the hospital, where the girl began to pray audibly. He said the words were beautiful, poetic and flowery. When she had finished she said to him, "Were the words not lovely?" And he replied, "Yes, my dear, they were." On their way down from the ward, his sister turned to him saying, "Mother hasn't got a chance, poor thing. She will die shortly." He told me how stunned he was with surprise.

Here is a perfect illustration of what this verse means. Love is Freedom. The words used by this good lady were beautiful and she was sincere enough in her own way. Nevertheless, they were as sounding brass and tinkling cymbal. In order to make words effective, they have to be felt as true. It is necessary to pour life, love and feeling into our words and statements of truth.

This girl had not Charity (Love). Charity, in the Bible, means Love. Love is the cement that binds. It is that sense of Oneness with the Father of all—the Almighty Power. Therefore, Love being a deep sense of our unity with God, with Life, with the All Powerful, we must in prayer become one with our ideal of perfection.

In the case of a woman who is sick in the hospital, we must not "see" her sick or in pain. No, we must have Charity—or Love—and see her as the perfect being, an offspring of the Infinite, clothed with all the qualities and attributes of God.

Love frees, it opens prison doors, sets free the captives and them that are bound. It gives beauty for ashes, the oil of Joy for mourning and the garment of praise for the spirit of heaviness that we may become trees of righteousness.

A simple treatment used by a son for his crippled mother in Rochester recently was as follows: He did not see her as a cripple—he had Charity, which is the Love of God, or Good. This boy healed his belief about his mother through Divine Love. He decided that he would become as a little child and shed all his preconceived notions and beliefs about medicine, doctors' verdicts, mother's attitude, etc. Twice daily he prayed in this simple, direct and spontaneous manner: "Mother's life is God's life and it flows through her now as harmony, health and peace. There is only the One Life and that is God and God is Life." Then he would say to himself, "How can the flow of life be impeded?" And he reasoned that, "In Truth it cannot be. Mother is believing a lie and she is experiencing the results of her false belief. Now," he said to himself, "the truth is God walks and talks in her. She is healed; made whole and perfect now—this instant!"

Then every night before going to sleep, in his imagination he would kiss his mother and feel her warm embrace. He would hear her say to him, "Son, a miracle has happened. God has healed me and I walk. Isn't it wonderful?" He would reply, "Yes, mother, His Name is wonderful!" Then he would go off to sleep into the arms of the Absolute Lover.

Truly this man spoke with the tongues of angels. The angel means the new attitude of mind, a new perception of God or Good. The angel is "the angle" at which we look at God. This boy's angle was that there is only One Presence and One Power and It is now moving in his behalf. "None shall stay its hand and say unto it what doest thou." Love frees.

# Chapter 3

❥ • • • • • • • • • • ❦

"And though I have the gift of prophecy, and understand all mysteries, and all knowledge; and though
I have all faith, so that I could remove mountains,
and have not charity I am nothing."

—(I Cor. 13:2)

Love is that subtle emanation that streams forth
from man wherein he has a feeling of oneness with
all life. Many people are gifted in countless ways, but
often there is something lacking.

They fail to radiate the mood of peace, harmony
and love.

When we see the growing corn, grass, trees, fruit
and buds on the branches, and when we observe the
sheep and cattle grazing in the valley, or when we hear
the song and laughter of children at play—all these
should remind us of the love of God. Infinite Providence is running the show and we can rest assured
that Love rules the world. Although men cannot see

God and live, they may look upon His Cosmos and His works and if they seek Him, they shall find.

If man seeks for love in the other, he will find it. Therefore, if we look rightly at the world we shall find the abundant life spoken of by Jesus. The world represents God thinking. Love is a symbol of the One-ness of God, and life, and all things.

It is the urge of all entities to go back to the Source. The journey back to God is the road back from relative love in this plane to the ultimate—or Absolute Lover—God. All the forms in the world that we see are simply an infinite variety of the thoughts of the One, the Beautiful and the Good. Love sustains and ensouls them all, for it is the Universal Solvent or solution which binds all things together in harmony, order and symmetry.

There is nothing but beauty in the world. Every atom of space is of indescribable beauty because God is Beauty. Moreover, every atom in space dances to the rhythm of the gods. The stars, the planets and the earth on which we move are purely symbols of the bow in the sky portraying God's covenant with all men whereby He sets forth order, precision and proportion.

The world and all things contained therein is the language of God in His handwriting. He that hath an ear let him hear and he will become still and listen.

He will hear the music of the spheres. He will understand the profundities of the Law and when he looks out upon the world he will see and hear differently. He will realize that all men are garments of God which He wears as he moves through the illusion of time and space and that all of us are on a journey of self-discovery.

All the stars, suns, moons, seas, mountains and all things we behold are symbols of still greater things—the archetypes of a transcendent perfection, witnesses of Truth—the same yesterday, today and forever. Therefore, if we are very smart and intelligent in the ways of the world even though we may write great works admired by all the world—all this is empty if we have not love in our hearts. Honor is not of man, it is of God. It is like the soldier in the recent war who won so many honors for his valor and prowess in battle. His chest was covered with medals and everyone thought he was most happy and proud. Yet at one of the ceremonies in his honor, he confided to friends, "All this means nothing to me; all I want is the love of the girl who no longer wants me. I love her and want to be loved by her." His heart was hungry and he knew instinctively and intuitively that pinning medals on him for killing other human beings was not the Love of God. He must have felt that we cannot live until we love, and love must have an object.

Live in livingness and givingness. It is the outward flow of life—and this flow must be harmonious, joyous, rhythmic and peaceful. This cosmic urge must be expressed in a positive, constructive manner. Man must be in tune with the Infinite. He must find the thing he loves to do in life and then do it. Then he is happy. This brings with it a sense of freedom and joyous expectancy. Such a man no longer watches the clock. His joy is in accomplishment and service. His work is not drudgery now. It is a pleasure.

A man recently chatted with the author aboard a plane. This man is considered a great prophet. Many of his prophecies have come true in recent years. He is an internationally known writer. He has great faith in himself and has made remarkable demonstrations. Yet he openly confessed his antagonism to members of a certain race, and was very bitter toward them.

However, as you see in the second verse of I Corinthians, 13th Chapter, even though he had all these wonderful gifts, he had not love. Therefore, it says, "I am nothing." "In Him there is no Greek, no Jew, no bond, no free, no male or female." Love knows no barriers of race or creed. Love is universal—it frees, it gives. It is the Spirit of God or Goodness, Truth and Beauty. This man admitted he lacked this impersonal love which is peace on earth and good will to all men.

We must love everyone. This we must do. We do not have to like them. The love spoken of is in this wise—we rejoice that all men are growing righteously, that the peace of God fills their souls and that they are being prospered in mind, body and affairs. We are glad the Law of God or Good is working for them, through them and around them.

This is love or that impersonal good will which we should radiate to all beings. It is like a fire in the kitchen, the warmth or glow from the coals does not favor but one side of the room. It shows no favoritism. It gives its heat to all, be they who they may. It has neither height nor depth, it neither comes nor goes, it fills all space, "IT IS". The ancients called it Love. God is Love. There is no true happiness and I am as nothing, until I learn to love and practice the presence of God. I begin to live life joyously when I see "sermons in stones, tongues in trees, songs in running brooks and God in everything."

# Chapter 4

*"And though I bestow all my goods to feed the poor, and though I give my body to be burned, and have not charity, is profiteth me nothing."*

—(I Cor. 13:3)

Let us explain this verse by the following true story. A woman came to the author about four years ago when he was lecturing at the Park Central Hotel in New York City and said to him, "I work for the Red Cross every day, I give money to all charitable organizations, and belong to the Sewing Club. I visit hospitals and conduct drives for veterans, etc. Yet misfortune after misfortune comes to me. Look at my fingers. They are inflamed and I can't take the rings off. The doctor calls it rheumatoid arthritis. Why? Why? I love so much and give so much!"

But, actually she had not love and so it profited her nothing. After talking with her a little while I discovered she wanted to be praised by the multitude.

She wanted her picture in the paper. She craved the flattering remarks of her associates. She forgot the common caution, "Let not your right hand know what your left hand doeth." Verily, they shall have their reward. Which means, yes, man will receive the praise of man—they will say what a fine fellow he is, how generous he is, how unselfish. And this satisfies the ego of the worldly-minded man. "But there is no reward of my Father in Heaven."

This woman's acts, though well-intentioned and good, were not really of the heart. She did not do these things for the joy and love of doing them and for the thrill of making others happy, joyous and free. Her motives were not pure and holy. She forgot there is no honor or glory of man. All honor and glory comes from God. Let us always examine our motives.

In the case of the woman cited, she was thinking in terms of lack and limitation and when she gave her gifts she was looking forward to tragedy, pain, cyclones and misfortunes of all kinds. This is absolutely wrong and certainly cannot be called Divine Love. Oftentimes people will do something for another and then say, "Aren't you grateful?" You see, then they are expecting something in return—and if I am grateful to you, I am under an obligation to you. When we do something for another, if it is what we call a love gift, then we should not place the other under any obligation whatever. "And though I give my body to be burned."

When this woman gave a gift, did some work for the Red Cross or any charitable organization it should have been done freely, gladly and for the joy of giving, expecting nothing in return. If she gave a gift and expected something in return it was not a gift. The gift of love has "no strings" of any nature whatever attached to it. It is as free as the wind. A gift given in this manner—whether work, service, money, or thoughts—comes back a thousand fold, pressed down, shaken together and running over. Let me cite another case I treated some years ago. A very possessive mother (thirty years in Truth) came to me complaining that she had scrubbed floors in order to send her daughter to a finishing school where she could become a little lady like the other girls in the neighborhood.

"I worked my fingers to the bone. I pinched pennies and sold rings which my dead husband had given me. And what do you think this ungrateful daughter did? She ran off and married a young doctor and they have gone to South Africa! She never even sent me a postcard. I'm so mad I could choke her!" I asked her what she had expected her daughter to do. "Well," she said, "after all I did for her I expected her to come home and wait on me in my old age, get a job and support me. Or if she got married to a rich man I would expect her to take me with her and live with her. You see, my daughter needs me and I love her so!" I healed, or rather my explanation of the Truth, healed this woman and she went off smiling with the radiance of the Light Limitless shining out through her eyes.

I explained to her that if she really loved her daughter, she would rejoice in her new found happiness and pray for her by knowing that love ensouls her, surrounds her and permeates every atom of her being. Moreover, that if she loved her daughter instead of feeling "burnt up", and instead of giving her body (her idea) of her daughter to be burned—in other words entertaining the idea of resentment—she should send love forth. The mood or feeling of love and peace for the daughter would automatically remove the feeling of resentment.

Love casts out hate. Hate and love cannot dwell together. "Perfect love casteth out fear." Hate is fear. She realized that love is freedom and that if she really loved her child, she would free her in the arms of God, knowing that Divine Love goes before her daughter to make safe and instant and perfect her way. She understood also that having done all she did for the girl was a labor of love and that she rejoiced doing it just because it was good and very good. She rejoiced in seeing her daughter grow up radiating peace, health and happiness.

Moreover, to love her daughter meant to "loose her and let her go", knowing that God is her father and God is her mother also, and God is round about her. She "saw the point" and rejoiced in her daughter's new found freedom. She was happy because her daughter was happy. She wired her congratulations and prayed sincerely from the heart for her peace and security and integrity.

What is harmony for the part is harmony for the whole, because the whole is in the part and the part is in the whole. Therefore, common sense dictates that in the case of this young daughter, love came on the scene. It was right, good and true that she accept it. This was the harmony of the part—and so it was harmonious for the mother and right for everyone in the world. Moreover, by its very nature it could only bless and make others happier. Instead of depriving the mother of anything, this realization of love and harmony for the good fortune of the daughter would bring blessings manifold to the mother.

To love is to release. "What I love I release, what I hate I bind." Mothers must be like the mother bird. When her young are ready to fly, she pushes them out of the nest and they learn to fly themselves. Mothers must give up this possessive attitude towards daughters and sons. They must cease thinking that they know best.

Parents must teach their children the Truth of Being—teach them how to pray successfully and scientifically and to stand on their own feet. Mothers must not expect their daughters to sacrifice home and children of their own just to stay with them and feel sorry for them. This attitude of mind on the part of child and parent has caused endless confusion and blighted the lives of many thousands.

This is why He said, "Leave father, mother, brother and sister and follow me." Yes, the "me" is the Truth. Truth is the way, the life, the quest and the goal. Truth brings good tidings to the meek, binds the broken hearted and proclaims liberty to the captives. Mothers and fathers must never worry about their children. This is a mood of fear, lack and limitation, and if the children do not know the laws of life they get the vibration or feeling of the parents and it drags them down.

The blind lead the blind and they both fall into the ditch. "I was young; now I am old. Yet never have I seen the righteous forsaken and their seed beg bread." (37th Psalm.) This means that if parents live the Truth, they will see their children as noble, dignified, Christlike beings. They will have the conviction that their children are growing righteously, and according to their conviction will it be done unto them.

They will clothe their children in the garment of salvation and the robe of righteousness. Their children then will never beg bread—meaning they will never do anything to dishonor God or their parents. They will truly grow in the image and likeness of the mood or conviction held by the parents. The parents clothed them with Divine Love. The aura of God ensouled them, encompassed them, fed them. Surely they could reflect only love.

"What thou seest, that too become thou must; God if thou seest God, dust if thou seest dust." Having seen and felt love for their children, the latter must reflect it by an inexorable, changeless law—which is, "Seek and you shall find." See God or Love coming forth in your children.

# Chapter 5

*"Charity suffereth long, and is kind; charity envieth not; charity vaunteth not itself, is not puffed up."*
—(I Cor. 13:4)

Recently a man told a little girl that her father, who had made the transition, had gone on a trip and that she would see him again in the future. Others criticized this man and said he lied.

No, he did not lie. He did the kind thing and made the girl happy. Moreover, what he said was true. Her father had made a journey in consciousness to the fourth dimension, and through love the child will again see him and talk with him. They will both play, as Dunne says, in the symphony of all creation.

Charity suffereth long and is kind. Yes, love endures forever. It is indissoluble. Nothing breaks it up or severs it because it is a quality or attribute of God—the same yesterday, today and forever. It is not changeable and variable. Love is, and all there is love. When we do the kind thing it is always love in action.

Let us ask ourselves what is the kind thing to say or do—this is the Truth.

Charity envieth not. The man who knows the laws of life never envies another. Neither is he jealous, because he knows that he can go to the same Fountain as the other and claim all the good that he wants. And if he believes, it shall be given him. A man, understanding this, cannot be jealous. He knows that God is impersonal and no respecter of persons.

"Come ye to the waters and drink. Yea, come ye, buy wine and milk, without money, without price." The only price we pay is belief, and belief costs nothing. Therefore, the qualities of mind in the other—his riches, his wife, his home or his estates—are not to be coveted. You, the reader, may also have any or all of these things by going to the same source as the other and ordering them.

"Regarding the works of my hand, command ye me." Your command is simply to appropriate the mood of possessing that which you desire and then rest in the Silence, knowing that what you prayed for is a fact in the Kingdom of Reality. Walking the earth in the light of this assumption, in the moment you think not it will appear as a quality of mind, object in space as a home, a wife, etc. "Vaunteth not itself." The sophisticated man, lacking knowledge of Truth, parades before himself time and again a whole procession of motives which he does not have, in order to conceal from himself that he is what he does not wish to be. He is proud, opinionated and arrogant. If he does a thing with an unworthy motive he claims it is a good one because it would shame him to recognize how bad the motive is. We must expose these spurious motives to ourselves and get rid of our false pride so that we can be proud of our relationship with God, the only Presence and the only Power. "Is not puffed up." We must get rid of the sense of our own importance, pride of rank, class distinction, or family tree. We must rid ourselves of this false intellectual pride. The great man is always the humble man. The greatest doctor is usually gentle, kind, loving and understanding.

The really great mystic is the humble man, knowing that all wisdom, power and intelligence comes from the One—the Father of all. So when he says "Our Father," he means it. He knows we have a common Father and that we are all brothers and sisters. He also knows we are descended from the Royal Family, that we have the greatest family tree in the world—I AM.

Yes, the tree of Life is in the midst of the Garden of God. This is the one indivisible tree and all members of the human family eat, live and have their being rooted in this Eternal Tree, fed by the sap that comes from the wisdom of the Father. It is the Christmas tree and we the children are gathered around to feast from the gifts—or manna—that falls from its branches.

The meal we eat is the realization of the Almighty Power; the bread we eat is the manna, or Divine Ideas that flow through us; the wine we drink is the inspiration from on High and the fruit we eat is the joy of the answered prayer. We know that Law waits on God and man, and that we are always sitting at the banquet table of God and that the feast is always prepared.

# Chapter 6

"*Doth not behave itself unseemly, seeketh not her own, is not easily provoked, thinketh no evil; rejoiceth not in iniquity, but rejoiceth in the truth.*"
—(I Cor. 13:5–6)

The one living in the consciousness of Love always does that which conforms to the good of all. He contributes to the betterment of society and never does anything that would disturb the harmony of the whole. His behaviour is always gentlemanly, courteous and kind. His presence is soothing, comforting and conducive to peace.

Wherever such a man goes he will always meet the White Brother, regardless of race or creed. He loves people, realizing God indwells all men so he is one with the God of All. Others, regardless of the color of their skin, sense this and respond in kind. "Seeketh not her own." If a man returns love to one that loves him, that is not enough. He must cease to be possessive in his love and let it become universal, so that his love for all men becomes all-inclusive.

A man must not behave unseemingly because his wife had dinner with another man. Neither should she hesitate to tell her husband about it. Love is freedom and also respect. If he truly loves his wife, he will trust her and have perfect faith in her honesty and integrity. He will not question her or "make a scene". No, he behaves as he should. He remains poised and calm, knowing that "Whom God hath joined together, no man can put asunder", which means their marriage was a spiritual union, "made in heaven", and therefore, no man or woman or power can break it up. This knowing and understanding is immediately felt by the wife and she responds in kind. She must remain true to his conviction of her.

What does he believe about his wife? Let him always see her as he first saw her. Let him always clothe her in the robe of glory and beauty, yea, the seamless robe. Let him say to his heart, "Thou art all fair my love, there is no spot on thee." Then she must reflect the Christ to him because he has seen and felt the Christ in her, "What thou seest, that thou beest."

Let me tell you the story of a woman who behaved herself unseemly. She was married, had two children and a devoted husband. They never quarreled. One day a gossiping neighbor said that she had seen the husband twice with a strange woman in a restaurant and that she thought he was "running around". The wife got so excited that she left her home, leaving a note with one of the children to give the father when he came home. Filled with rage and jealousy she ran off to Reno to get a divorce.

She obtained a Reno decree, never listening to any explanation offered by the husband. Months later she found out that the woman in question was her husband's sister, whom he was befriending. "Love is not easily provoked." She did not have the understanding of God, which is also Love . . . "thinketh no evil". Yes, if married people would cease suspecting each other, happiness would reign. A boy and girl get married. They seem to be the perfect couple. Yet oftentimes in a few months they are separated and divorced. Why? This, for example, may be one of the reasons. The young wife might visit her husband's office and see a pretty girl there. Some evening he might come home late.

Instead of trusting him, she begins to suspect him. Silently she begins to fear that he is going to "run around" and that he is not going to be faithful to her.

She says nothing to him, and since neither of them understand the laws of life, what she continues to fear comes to pass. Her conviction about him is communicated to him and he feels it subjectively. He becomes restless and does the thing she was convinced he would do. Then she becomes frantic and goes home to mother and the law-suit begins.

Love thinketh no evil. Love sees the Christ Truth always. Love is faithful to the end and the end is always good, because God is Good.

I have a letter from a woman in London who had been married twenty years when suddenly there was a flare-up and a break, and before she realized it they were on the verge of a divorce. People told her that her husband was running around with other women, and he was. She said nothing but this is what she did. She prayed that her husband be divinely guided in thought and action and that only right action prevail. She loosed him and let him go, realizing that the love of God flowed through his thoughts, words and deeds, that peace filled his soul and that Infinite Spirit revealed to him the perfect way of life. "I am the way, the truth and the life."

He gave up the other women and came back to her in love and peace. She was a wise woman. She knew that love frees and that his happiness was her happiness. She gave him an impersonal treatment, rejoicing that all good was his now, not telling God what to do but rather realizing the truth about it. It was a perfect demonstration of the healing power of love. Love joined them together. How could anyone sever that love? They could not if it were real love, for real love is almighty and indivisible. Who can sever it?

"Rejoiceth not in iniquity, but rejoiceth in the truth." The Truth student or the Christian (the latter word means anyone that practices the principle of Truth) never rejoices that a nation is vanquished. Never, under any circumstances, does he have a desire "to get even" or rejoice over the misfortunes of others. Iniquity means unbalance, lack of firm balance or equilibrium. The Truth student never listens to anything that will not contribute to his good or the good of another.

Some people, through gross ignorance, seem to rejoice in gossiping about others, attacking their character, backbiting, etc. To talk about and dwell upon the imperfections of another (whether true or false) is to attract limitation and loss to oneself. The Law is "As you would that men should talk about you, speak you also about them in like manner." This is the rule of a free, happy life. The person who spreads spicy gossip is thinking it and feeling it, so what is going to happen? It is easy to answer: "As a man thinketh in his heart, so is he." To imagine evil of another is to lie.

Let us rejoice in the Truth now that all men are expressing the truth. The Truth is God indwells each man and let us bear witness to that truth by knowing that those who would criticize and condemn *are now dramatizing, portraying and expressing love, peace and harmony.* Once a thief came to murder a man but the man's little daughter *did not see* a murderer. She saw a "nice" man who maybe would give her candy. She played with his trousers and sang for him. He left with tears in his eyes and was healed. Love rejoices in the Truth.

# Chapter 7

⋙ · · · · · · · · · ⋘

*"Beareth all things, believeth all things, hopeth all things, endureth all things. Charity never faileth: but whether there be prophecies, they shall fail; whether there be tongues, they shall cease; whether there be knowledge, it shall vanish away."*

—(I Cor. 13:7–8)

Love creates and gives birth to all forms. For example, when two forces such as hydrogen and oxygen meet, water forms. Love, likewise, is a union, an emotional attachment. Love is the cement that binds. Let us become one with our ideal by loving it, then we will give birth to the new man. Truly love beareth all things. When we treat or pray, we must have love in our hearts because we must accept as true that which our five senses deny. This is real love also. Love is the fulfilling of the law. When we are so convinced of the Truth which we affirm, there is no room for the opposite.

The man with love in his heart does bear the so-called burdens of the world on his shoulders because he knows wisdom rules the world, and that an Infinite Providence guides it on its course. The man of understanding knows that all men—beggar, thief and holy man—shall, at their appointed time, come to see the transcendent glory which He is.

No one is lost—there is no such thing as a lost soul. God cannot lose himself, neither can he destroy himself. "They shall not hurt nor destroy in all my Holy Mountain." (Isaiah 11:9) Hope springs eternal in the breast of the Truth student, but this hope is an abiding faith in an omnipresent and ultimate good.

The mental scientist endureth all things in this sense. He knows that whatever problem presents itself to him, that God has the answer. He, therefore, casts his burden on the Christ within, which means the Truth—i.e., he does not take the problem to God because Infinite Intelligence has no problem. He goes to God with the answer. Behold God flows through his problem and there is no problem.

The sincere Truth student is not weighed down by problems and vexations of the day. He refuses to bear these burdens. He knows there is a way out and his joy is in overcoming his problem. He knows that the so-called trials which beset him are his opportunities to discover the God-power within. He tastes God and he finds Him good. He has become acquainted with the one Power. Therefore, he walks along the highway of life smiling, a song in his heart—the song of the Lamb (Victory). If the crossword puzzle was all figured out for man and he were asked just to fill in the blank spaces, life would be drab. No, the thrill of accomplishment comes in working out the problem. The engineer rejoices in building a bridge where others failed. There is great satisfaction in overcoming. We are here to prove our Divinity, so we endure all things and experiences gladly, knowing that he who perseveres to the end shall be saved. This means that man, instead of attacking and fighting his problems, simply lets go and becomes still and says to the Father within, "Now Father, this is what I want. The right answer is mine now. Infinite Intelligence has revealed it to me now. Thank you Father." If a man will say this silently or audibly to himself (because prayer is basically man talking to his higher self), and say it knowingly and feelingly, the answer will come and bring peace with it.

Man is here to discover the joy of living and awaken from his dream of limitation to claim his sonship. He can use the law of life two ways. "I form the light, and create darkness: I make peace, and create evil: I, the Lord do all these things." (Isaiah 45:7) When he gets tired using the law of life negatively—in other words, when he is tired of being "pushed around"—he begins to ask questions about why, where, whence and whither. Then his dissatisfaction leads to satisfaction and he deduces a law from all his experiences. The thrill is in discovery. The reader of this book would not give up his unpleasant experiences. I'll wager each man is glad he has had them even though they were unpleasant, because through them he found the Light. "Sweet are the uses of adversity, like a toad, ugly and venomous, yet wears a precious jewel in his head."

Man's extremity is God's opportunity. We do not have to suffer, but we undergo pain and misery due to our ignorance. As Emerson says, the only sin is ignorance and the only punishment the inevitable consequence. When man truly finds God, he becomes serene, poised, balanced. He has found that to be in tune with the Infinite is to discover that all His ways are pleasantness and all his paths are peace.

Here in the objective world we are conscious of opposites, such as north and south, night and day, male and female, cold and heat, love and its opposite, joy and sorrow. How would we know what love was except we were able to shed a tear of sorrow! Opposites are necessary for our growth so that all of us may experience the joy and significance of positives. The positive affirmative attitude towards life, believing in all good things, is what Quimby called Christ. Christ is the wisdom which Jesus, Moses, Buddha and the illumined mystics found. This wisdom is the knowledge of God and the way He works. Then, knowing the law of life we apply it scientifically, wisely and judiciously to bless ourselves and others.

We have found that the opposites are not irreconcilable. We can always go to the Garden of God or the Holy of Holies within ourselves and pray, believing that peace, health, harmony and happiness are ours just for the asking. God is the gift and also the giver. Man is the receiver. Our prayer, therefore, is walking in the light of the assumption that our prayer is already answered. We know it exists in the Kingdom of Reality and if we wait yet a little while, it will appear on the screen of space.

Love never faileth. For how can God fail? The predictions, statements and idle talk of men fail, but the consciousness of love protects, guides, guards and illumines man. The love spoken of here is the inner silent knowing, a movement of consciousness, welling up from the heart. The consciousness of being one with your ideal will win. This is the mood that demonstrates. The mood of love or oneness with your ideal never faileth. This power, or mental attitude is omnipotent, because it is the spirit of God moving in your behalf. It is the formless moving into objectivity.

It is true that the prophecies of men fail, because these many times are based on the evidences of the senses, race belief, doctors' verdicts and scientific facts dependent upon objective analysis. But to this subjective self of man "All things are possible". Therefore, if he will not judge according to appearances (prophecies of man) but only believe that the God-power has fulfilled his request and then rest in that conviction, he will find that love (oneness with his idea) never faileth.

"Whether there be tongues they shall cease." Man, in a hospital bed, crying with pain, is speaking in the tongue or mood of limitation and lack. He does not know God or Truth, because to know Truth is to be free. Hence, this tongue or mood of lack must cease and he must change his consciousness. It is of no use to pray to God and at the same time believe that some other power can overturn, neutralize or destroy the action of God. This form of prayer is useless. Moreover, it is a waste of energy.

We must remember that it is our inner feeling or mood that will be manifested regardless of all the statements of Truth that we use. Therefore, our affirmations or statements of Truth must be permeated with love, feeling and conviction. This mental attitude or state of consciousness is to pray believing, and according to our belief "it will be done unto us."

The consciousness or feeling of being healed is the Almighty Power that heals.

Let man close his eyes, think of God, then realize that all the God-like qualities and attributes are within himself. That his own consciousness or awareness is the Almighty Power that demonstrates and materializes. Let him now contemplate on the fact that he is healed and perfect. Let him rejoice that every tissue, muscle, bone, electron and atom of his being is now conforming to the pattern on the mount. Let him realize that the Holy Spirit, which moves through him now, is the Spirit of Omnipotence and that the spiritual man is now being revealed.

As man continues to do this he moves from fear and anxiety to the mood of love and peace. His fear is changed to the feeling of confidence in an Almighty Power which acts according to his feeling or belief. Then the tongue of man (limitation) ceases and the tongue of God (mood of love and peace) decrees triumphantly.

"Whether there be knowledge, it shall vanish away." Yea, the wisdom of man is foolishness in the eyes of God. All the pioneers, artists, inventors, scientists were at one time ridiculed by the world. They were considered dreamers, visionaries. The world said radio, electric lights, telephones, etc., were impossible, these and many other inventions being looked upon as impossible of practical achievement. Yet, the dreamers believed the unbelievable. They believed that the impossible was possible. They knew that love, a feeling of oneness, of conviction with man's good or ideal would win. Infinite Intelligence revealed the way.

# Chapter 8

*"For we know in part, and we prophesy in part. But when that which is perfect is come, then that which is in part shall be done away."*

—(I Cor. 13:9–10)

In John 3:2 we read, "Beloved now are we the sons of God and it doth not yet appear what we shall be, but we know that when he shall appear, we shall be like him for we shall see him as he is." We are here to awaken to our Divine perfection, and as we die to all our false beliefs and race concepts we will have purified our sub-conscious mind and then the Christ, the illumined man, will appear as the Anointed One. The conscious mind (Jesus) and the subconscious mind (Christ) will become one, united in perfect harmony. The two become one. Then the part is done away with, the limited man is now dead and the perfect man, the Christ, is revealed. We now see ourselves as sons of God in the bosom of the Father. We are awakened.

*"When I was a child, I spake as a child, I under-*
*stood as a child. I thought as a child: but when I*
*became a man, I put away childish things."*

—(I Cor. 13:11)

We must not be ruled by childish thought, nor by dead thoughts. Millions walk the earth, still in bondage to the beliefs and opinions accepted by them in their infancy or youth. Their childish belief in the boogie man under the stairs, or a devil with horns, or hell and damnation, all these foolish beliefs must be discarded. We must be governed by the idea of the Son of man or Son of God (The Truth).

Our governing idea must be that we are Sons of God. Therefore, we must have the same qualities and attributes and capacities as the Father. Let us go forth and make ourselves equal with God and we shall not feel it robbery to do the works of God. "He made himself equal with God and found it not robbery to do the Works of God." We must identify ourselves as one with the Father and cease to identify ourselves in consciousness with childish things, such as fearing and believing in things and powers that do not exist.

When a child becomes a man, he must cease transferring the power that is within himself to things outside himself. In other words, he must cease worshipping the false gods of sickness, disease, pain and poverty. He now knows the laws of life and that these things are brought on by man himself by his own wrong thinking, his fears, and false beliefs. Now the man knows he is a son of God and entitled to all good things; so he goes forth, claiming his sonship and finds that all his ways are pleasantness and all his paths are peace.

We must grow up in our love nature also. It would seem that we are very immature in our emotional nature. We must cease to be vain, arrogant and boastful. God is Love, therefore, love is good in all its forms and modifications. If we see faults in the husband or sister, it is not a part of love. Jealousy is a counterfeit phase and so is resentment.

Let us consider the following. A certain man objected to his wife's expressing herself as a creative artist. She could create new, attractive designs for hats. She wanted to take a position in a nearby establishment. The opportunity presented itself, yet the husband was so possessive that he said to her, "No, your place is in the home. Be there when I come back!" They had no children. She was frustrated and unhappy because she did not want to go against his wishes.

This man was ruled by a childish thought and did not know what love is. His idea of love had failed to grow up. Love is freedom and does not deny the right of expression to the other. If he really loved his wife, he would have daily encouraged her, rejoiced that she had found a measure of happiness in designing hats.

If I truly love the other, I want to see the other happy and prosperous. There is that Cosmic urge within us, constantly seeking to express itself at higher levels of consciousness. Man must never limit, circumscribe or put chains on love and say, "Your attention is to me only, never mind your artistic ability." This is selfishness based on fear of loss. Man loses what he will not let expand, grow and unfold.

This case ended up in the divorce court. The woman became a great artist and has contributed much to the world. She found her ideal husband through prayer and of course he encouraged her and brought out greater beauty than ever before.

The sense of personal freedom held by husband and wife portray the real spiritual marriage, wherein each is wedded to God (Good), and one with Him in livingness and givingness. Wives and husbands should learn to free each other instead of binding one another. Then they have truly grown up and have put away childish thoughts. The love of God in their thoughts, words and deeds will guide them in all their ways. His name is "inscribed on their hearts and written in their inward parts."

Let us broaden our horizon and enlarge the borders of our tent, so that gradually our love becomes the love which Jesus had. His love was not limited to his mother, father or those around him. No, he loved all humanity. This is the universal love which includes the beggar and the holy man. Yes, even the thief on the cross.

We must realize that God is the Absolute Lover, the Impartial Universal Divine Giver. He gives to all men, regardless of creed and color, that which they feel as true of themselves. He never questions them and says, "What are you going to do with the thousand dollars you want?" God is the Giver and the Gift. Man is the receiver.

The love of woman for a man is a reciprocal mood in which the subjective nature of the woman is complemented by the objective nature of the man. She finds the image and likeness of her subjective desires in a man. Her subjective feeling realizes its objective fullness in a marriage "made in heaven" (spiritual consciousness).

Our understanding of God increases as we fail to see the parts and begin to see the underlying unity behind all things, a unity in diversity. Then love in action is the desire of diversity for unity. Our journey here is a journey back to the One and the glory which we had with Him before the world was. "Thou hast been in Eden, the Garden of God and the ruby was thy covering." When a man and a woman marry it brings them up further in the scale of unity.

# Chapter 9

*"For now we see through a glass, darkly; but then face to face: now I know in part; but then I know even as also I am known."*

—(I Cor. 13:12)

We cannot see without eyes, nor hear without ears, nor apprehend without the power of thinking. So the act of becoming the perfect man, here and now, would be impossible if the perfect ideal has not already been created within us. We see through a glass darkly now. We do not see this Divine Presence within us, which is absolute perfection, but we instinctively and intuitively sense something divine welling up within us.

Nature provides signs which indicate future happenings. Consider the fledgling before it flies in the air. It flutters and shakes its wings. This is a promise of its power to fly. The same process takes place in man. He reads the story of Jesus who awakened here on earth, who claimed His Oneness with God, translated his body and went back to dwell in the bosom of the Absolute Father like an arrow that is lost in its mark.

Men turn to God in prayer and adoration, which is a reverent or mystic awe in contemplating our own IAMness. In this meditative mood, man contemplates his good and rejoices in anticipation. Then he may be said to feel joy before joy, to feel beauty before beauty, to feel happiness before happiness. The tree about to bear fruit puts forth shoots, flowers and leaves in anticipation. Observe the vine, a piece of God's handicraft, with its tendrils, suckers, leaves and petals which speak to man their own language and proclaim their joy at the forthcoming fruit.

Likewise, the dawn appears and the shadows flee away. Let us become illumined by the Holy Spirit. This will lead the way to the birth of the Savior, because as Mary (the subjective) is constantly being impregnated by Christlike thoughts and ideals, the Garden of God is freed from all weeds. Then comes forth the Jesus Christ state of consciousness.

Each time we pray aright our prayer is answered. Then we see God (our good) face to face. When I see your face, I recognize you. Each time we turn to the Truth and recognize it, it recognizes us and we become one with the Truth and are free. It is the story of the prodigal who returns to his father (conscious mind realizing God-like powers within him and has the answer to all). The father does not condemn or criticise, but as the son turns to the father, the father turns to him and kisses him. He does not berate him or ask him why he ran away from home. No, he is the Absolute Lover who gives all and is no respector of persons. If we complain about our lot the answer is, "Son, thou art ever with me and all that I hath is thine."

The scripture says "The pure in heart shall see God." We are told that no man can see God and live. Whoever dwells on virtue and beauty sees virtue and beauty and sees God or Good. The pure in heart see God every day.

"Peace is the power at the heart of God." With peace in our hearts we sit at the banquet table of the Lord, presided over by the God of Love. God never forgets his children. When the children forget their Divine Origin and vainly search for their good elsewhere, they have a sense of separateness from God, but they have only to return to find themselves in the Changeless Presence that always indwells them. The love of God illumines the darkness. Let us smile, the smile of love to another illumines his heart.

All of us reflect the glory of God in some degree. When our thought is uplifted, we reflect His Glory. When the subjective state of our thought is governed solely by the Holy Spirit it reflects this reality in all that we say or do. "But then shall I know as also I am known." The reader is known now as the Son of God. "Beloved, now are we the Sons of God."

As the birth of God takes place in us by dying daily to all the false beliefs of the race and anointing all our thoughts with the Holy Spirit, we then come into the light of the Spirit and realize that God is within us, and the life of us all the time. As we go from glory to glory we will some day awaken and discover our inner self.

This higher self is now hidden, due to the darkness of our thought which covers it. As we wash the windows of our soul, the light and sunshine, inspiration and divine illumination will illumine us. Then we shall see spiritually. We can see only perfection, order, symmetry and proportion. We will see Divinity behind the form, the Truth behind the mask. Opposites will disappear and we will see only the Unity, or Oneness of all things.

We shall see ourselves as we really are, identities in the bosom of the Father, lights making up the one Great Light, the Absolute, the Silent, Brooding Presence, changeless and ageless, "Without beginning or end, older than night or day, younger than the babe newborn, brighter than light, darker than darkness, beyond all things and creatures, yet fixed in the heart of all of us." "Who is born of love is born of God, for God is Love." "Love is the fulfilling of the Law." "Much is forgiven him, because he hath loved much."

If a man is full of the Divine Fire, radiating that subtle essence of love to all, then to such a man all things are possible. His desires are fulfilled and the gift of God is made. This gift is the more abundant life, a celestial love and an abiding peace. We come close to the presence of "the Ancient of Days", through love that wells up in our hearts toward all men and our Father.

# Chapter 10

*"And now abideth faith, hope, charity, these three; but the greatest of these is charity."*

—(I Cor. 13:13)

**H**ope is the expectation of all good. The expectancy of the best is truly a great prayer. "Faith is the substance of things hoped for, the evidence of things not seen." Faith is your inner knowing or feeling of confidence or trust, containing within itself the mold of expression. Love is our union with our ideal, the fulfilling of the law. The law decrees that whatever we idealize and feel ourselves to be, the formless awareness within us takes form according to our belief. This is accomplished through love, which in prayer means becoming filled with the feeling of being what we long to be.

Loving our ideal and becoming one with it brings about that inner certitude or satisfaction that follows true prayer. Through Divine Love, a love for Truth and the mysteries of life, we perceive intuitively great truths without any process of reasoning. As we begin to contemplate our unity with Life, with God and with the Universe, we will become more and more aware of the Divine Presence.

We must experience Holy Communion frequently. This can be accomplished by disciplining our five senses, stilling the body and mind and realizing our communion with "He who is". "Speak to Him thou, for He hears." Sometimes man is blinded by this light of illumination. This is the Divine Fire spoken of by the mystics, which illumines the whole house (man's mind). In such a moment others present are dazzled by the radiance of the Light Limitless.

The illumined, or partially illumined man has had glimpses of reality and knows that man is immortal and his individuality endures forever. He knows that each person is a manifestation of the One Life and that whatever happens to one is impregnated and recorded in the universal subjectivity common to all of us.

The individual called John Jones is one of the many that make up God, for God is the one in many, and the streams of "manyness" are all flowing back to the Oneness where they sense this Oneness with the original stream, the Source. Having found the All, we think in terms of God and are His co-workers in the Grand Symphony of all Creation. We rejoice in the growth and unfoldment of all men. This is an attribute of God called Love, because what we possess is the possession of all. When I rejoice in the good fortune of my fellow man, good fortune comes to me. "For love never faileth." "This is the Divine Measure which is pressed down, shaken together and running over." In the same way when we criticise or injure another we injure ourselves. Why should we therefore not love, when the love we give to others we really give unto ourselves? Then comes our liberation and our freedom. Man himself is the giver, the gift and the receiver. Man's body is an idea in consciousness. Man's consciousness is called IAM. The IAM, for example, in Mary, Tom or Jack is the same that which says "I AM" in the reader. When we say "I AM", that is God. In Him we live, move and have our being. Let us, therefore, realize our essential unity. This is loving one another, or becoming one with each other in wisdom and understanding. Let us stop fighting shadows, the darkness of our minds, and let us realize that God is within. Let us turn to Him smilingly and say "Father, I have come home." As we become still, we will feel and sense the soft tread of the "Ancient of Days" and He will welcome us with a kiss of love. In His Presence we will discover that His life is the life of all our brothers and sisters in the Cosmos.

Contemplating this Divine Truth, we become every other creature, for they all say "I AM" in varying degrees. We have discovered that all other beings are extensions of ourselves, the One Self, our own I AM or Life, the reality of every creature. God is Life and His life is the reader's life and as long as God lives, the reader will live. God is that which was, is and shall be. Therefore, we live forever. Furthermore, we know that the planets are thoughts, that suns and moons are thoughts, and that our own consciousness is the reality which sustains them all. Temporarily, in space, are moving the dreams of the dreamer and the Cosmos and all things therein contained are thoughts of the thinker. We have touched the All and He is meditating and we are His meditation. It is our own consciousness meditating on the mysteries of itself.

The student of Truth, having had a glimpse of Reality is no longer full of fears and forebodings. He does not fear life, nor death, nor anything in the past, present or future. Love has cast out all fear. He throws off the old garments of pride, the arrogance and tinsel of his creeds, dogmas and superstition. He now knows the Glory from on High, and feels and realizes that he dwells in eternity. He knows that once upon a time his own consciousness, that thing within him which makes him say "Father", moved upon the face of the waters and said "Let there be light." Moreover, he

knows that following the desire of his own consciousness "All the stars sang together and the Sons of God
shouted for joy."

Yes, man has played all roles, has been everywhere
and seen everything. Furthermore, the I AM in man
created everything. "Where wast thou when I laid the
foundations of the earth." We are God, walking the
earth in a dream of limitation, and we have forgotten our Divine Origin. Yet, when we awaken, we find
that the whole world is a projection of the thought of
our deep self. Only in Truth is there Divine Freedom.
Only in God is there power.

We are dwelling in Eternity now, immortal beings,
and in order that we may bring the love of God to all
men, let us rebuild our temple in the silence, without
"sound of hammer" or "voice of workmen". Let us
enthrone in our mind a government of divine ideas,
mothered by the Holy Spirit. This will be a government of the wise. Our tomorrows are the reflections
of our todays. Yes, they are the image and likeness of
today. God is the Eternal Now. "Now is the day of salvation."

Let us live lovingly today and the pulse beat of
the Holy Mother that throbs in us today, will animate
ourselves and those around us tomorrow. The mood
of love that emanates from us now, will speak through
the boys and girls of a generation yet unborn. We shall

one day read their words, which will be "apples of gold in pictures of silver", to God, which is our true self, that which is to be, which must be. Now, let us this day consecrate and dedicate our thoughts and feelings. Let us become clothed with immortality and the Garment of Love. The Song of the Lamb now wells up in our hearts, the angels and the archangels join us in the Celestial Choir and Jesus, the Great Conductor, leads, and all of us, through Love, are now playing in the Divine Orchestra. "And yet another commandment I give unto you. Love ye one another."

# Chapter 11

"The Pharisees also came unto him, tempting him, and saying unto him, 'Is it lawful for a man to put away his wife for every cause?'

"And he answered and said unto them, 'Have ye not read, that he which made them at the beginning made them male and female?'

"'And said, For this cause shall a man leave father and mother, and shall cleave to his wife: and they twain shall be one flesh? Wherefore they are no more twain, but one flesh.

"'What therefore God hath joined together, let not man put asunder.'

"They say unto him, 'Why did Moses then command to give a writing of divorcement and put her away?'

*"He saith unto him, 'Moses because of the hardness of your hearts suffered you to put away your wives: but from the beginning it was not so.*

*"'And I say unto you, Whosoever shall put away his wife, except it be for fornication, and shall marry another, committeth adultery: and whoso marrieth her which is put away doth commit adultery.'*

*"His disciples say unto him, 'If the case of the man be so with his wife, it is not good to marry.'*

*"But he said unto them, 'All men cannot receive this saying, save they to whom it is given.*

*"'For there are some eunuchs, which were so born from their mother's womb: and there are some eunuchs which were made eunuchs of men: and there be eunuchs, which have made themselves eunuchs for the kingdom of heaven's sake. He that is able to receive it, let him receive it'."*

—(Matthew 19:3–12)

Have ye not read that he which made them at the beginning made them male and female?" This refers to the dual aspect of consciousness—the two phases or functions of mind, namely, the conscious and sub-conscious. The conscious is referred to as the male and the subconscious as the female aspect of creation.

The conscious mind is personal and selective; the subconscious mind is impersonal and nonselective. The conscious mind has the power to impress ideas and concepts on the subconscious mind through feel-ing. The subconscious mind receives all ideas felt as true and gives form and expression to them in its own way, by "ways ye know not of."

Knowing this to be true, the truth student or men-tal scientist is very careful of the thoughts he chooses. For when we dwell on a particular idea or concept of ourselves, we find our emotional nature becoming stirred either positively or negatively. It is the law of life that any idea—good, bad or indifferent—which is emotionalized becomes subjectified, and in due course objectified. When we realize this, we will become very careful of our moods and feelings.

Our moods give birth to our children (conditions, events, circumstances, etc.) Children possess the qual-ities of the parents. We must be very careful, there-fore, that the mother (mood or feeling) of our children is pure and holy.

"For this cause shall a man leave father and mother, and shall cleave to his wife: and they twain shall be one flesh." Yes, man must leave father and mother, which means the old beliefs, superstitions and race thoughts. He must no longer have false gods such as fear, doubt, worry, resentment, etc. He must not look to the world for peace, guidance, illumination, supply or strength.

Rather must he look to the God within—the source of all supply whose bounty is ever present. His faith must not be in his father or mother, friend or brother. His faith and reliance must be on the Indwelling Christ, Emmanuel—the God in us—his own I AMness. Only then is his faith well founded for "HE that loveth father and mother more than me is not worthy of me."

Man likes to cling to his old creeds, dogmas and doctrines for sentimental reasons only. Though he has outgrown the old concept of things, yet for social, political or family reasons, he hesitates to throw them away and consecrate himself solely to the Truth of Being. Such a man has a conflict in consciousness and cannot have a full realization of the Presence of God. There is a quarrel in his consciousness—his false pride causing him to refuse the Truth which sets him free.

"Man shall cleave to his wife." This means man must be true to his ideal—his desired objective—by consciously claiming himself to be that which he longs to be, and feeling the reality of his desire. Man must not permit himself to react negatively to suggestions of fear, lack or doubt. For such suggestions, if entertained or believed, become conditions in his world. No, he remains faithful to his beloved (ideal, desire).

"They twain shall become one flesh." In prayer, when man withdraws from the world and contemplates the joy and happiness that would be his on realizing his objective, he enters into a fixed psychological state. Now he has become one in consciousness with his defined objective or ideal and he is at peace. Now the two (man and his desire) have become one. His inner feeling of joy indicates that he has passed over from the former state to the present state of consciousness.

Man's bride or wife is his concept of himself. She should be a bride of the Lord, a noble, dignified, Christ-like state of consciousness. Let us cleave to this state of consciousness and contrive to sustain it until we are married to it. As we grow from glory to glory we will reach the Jesus Christ state of consciousness.

"What God hath joined together, let no man put asunder." When man reaches the absolute conviction that his prayer is answered, or that the other is healed, and this conviction is unshakable, then God has joined them together and the two become one. The spiritual man knows that the subjective embodiment must come forth in the scope of spiritual creative activity. This spiritual issue is inevitable.

"They say unto him, 'Why did Moses then command to give a writing of divorcement, and put her away?'" Moses here refers to a state of consciousness whereby man subscribes to man-made laws, and is schooled in unholy beliefs.

The creeds and beliefs of the world are mostly determined by the flesh rather than the Spirit. This worldly, materialistic minded individual wedded to his past does not know that God is within him and that his own unconditioned Consciousness or awareness of Life is God. Neither does he know that the solution to all problems is within him. Inasmuch as his desires for peace, happiness, security and integrity come from within himself, if he knew the law of life he would accept these desires in free and unconditioned consciousness and Infinite Intelligence would bring them to pass.

Man, not knowing the law, rejects these desires and ideas that come to him as being impossible. He says, "I'm too old, don't have the right connections, haven't sufficient money, etc." He sets up thousands of reasons why he can't realize the cherished desires of his heart. Therefore, he gives these ideas and aspirations that well up with him "a writing of divorcement" and puts them away.

This rejection is due to his ignorance. He does not know there is a power within him which is capable of bringing all things to pass, and "None shall stay its hand and say unto it, What dost thou?" Moreover, asleep within man and merely waiting his recognition and claim are inspiration, divine guidance, and illumination. These too he puts away due to ignorance and seeks his guidance from the world.

So the Scripture says that "Moses out of the hardness of your heart suffered you to put away your wives." This refers to the man whose concept of God is that of a tyrannical Being living in the skies. He makes a God out of his own imagination and says that He is a God of vengeance and caprice—a Being who plays favorites, a sort of horrendous creature that we can't depend on since he might at any moment send a cyclone, tornado or earthquake.

Man's concept of God hardens his heart. When he awakens and finds out that the subjective self or Life in himself is God, then he leaves the Moses state of consciousness which represents the state of mental development relative to the law of his being from the negative side. He is now beginning to learn of Truths and comes out from the maze of old theological concepts of existence. The exact opposite of man-made laws is most often true and "fact" evidence is oftentimes false.

"Whosoever shall put away his wife, except it be for fornication, and shall marry another, committeth adultery: and whoso marrieth her which is put away doth commit adultery." This is easy to interpret if we will dispense with these silly, outlandish ideas that God instituted marriage laws and that we must adhere to the letter of them.

God never instituted any marriage laws. All the ceremonies and rituals that we have today are all man-made and vary in every part of the world. Obviously, God couldn't have all these conflicting and varying ideas about marriage. "In Him there is no Greek, no Jew, no bond, no free, no male, no female." "In Heaven there is no marriage or giving and taking in marriage."

The adultery spoken of in this verse means idolatry—the worship of false gods. For example, if man gives power to any external condition, he is adulterating his thought. He is, in effect, implying that the God Power in him does not have the power to overcome the circumstance or condition. In other words, he is becoming charged with fear, and fear is a lack of faith in God.

If a man conditions the realization of his desire on external conditions, he is adulterating his thought. If a man conditions the realization of his desire on money, influences, etc., he is adulterating his thought. He is saying, "I have to help God out." If he begins to wonder when, where, how and through what source, he is also an adulterer. Therefore, when we put away our wife (our highest ideal) and marry or become one with fear, doubt, hate, sense of failure or dependency on others, we have "committed adultery."

"And whosoever marrieth her that is put away committeth adultery." Yes, if man begins to broadcast his prayer of supplication and beseeching to a God in space somewhere, he is postulating a God outside himself and has a sense of separateness. "He marries her that is put away and likewise commits adultery." This belief in a God apart from man is false, hence an adulterated concept. He is never sure whether God will hear the broadcast or not. He has no way of knowing. Such a man is begging God as if He were hard hearted—he is cringing before Him as though God were withholding.

"God is the Gift and the Giver." "I am a gift unto you." "Come ye to the waters and drink, Yea come ye, buy wine and milk without money and without price." The only price for all divine gifts, be they what they may, is "belief." It costs nothing. No one can make you believe something that you don't want to, for there are no conditions or specifications laid down. "Canst thou believe?" "All things are possible to him that believeth."

"His disciples say unto him, 'If the case of the man be so with his wife, it is not good to marry.'" The disciples are our attitudes of mind, our twelve faculties. In most cases they are not disciplined and are governed by world beliefs. So the worldly man cannot understand that that which he marries is a state of consciousness, his own mental concept.

He finds it difficult to believe that his wife is that which he is conscious of being, his dominant mental attitude. He finds it hard to comprehend that the conscious state in which he dwells is his wife or mother of his children. Their children are his body, affairs, finances, health, etc. So man, looking out into the world says, "It is not good to marry. There is so much divorce, separation, and unhappiness." He looks upon marriage as a game of chance, not knowing that he attracts to himself a wife, conditioned exactly upon his inner mood or conviction.

"But he said unto them, 'All men cannot receive this saying, save they to whom it is given.'" All men cannot see this Truth. They believe in chance, coincidence, accidents, good luck and bad luck. They cannot receive the saying "all is Law and all is Love." There is only Law and there can't be chance, coincidence or bad luck in a world ruled by Law.

An unhappy marriage or divorce is a perfect working out of a given state of consciousness. It simply is the external manifestation of the discord in the man and his wife. Therefore, it is good and very good—a perfect working of a Law which never changes, which plays no favorites. We see a part of the process and condemn it, but if we could see spiritually we would see the perfect ending. "All men shall see the transcendent glory which I am." When we learn that the law is really one of freedom and cooperate with it, then we find it is a Law of Love.

"For there are some eunuchs which were so born from their mother's womb: and there are some eunuchs which were made eunuchs of men: and there be eunuchs, which have made themselves eunuchs for the Kingdom of Heaven's sake. He that is able to receive it, let him receive it." Eunuchs are our desires, concepts or ideals which are asleep or dead within us. We are eunuchs when we fail to animate and realize our God given desires.

We are here to radiate peace, love, and happiness. In other words, as Sons of God we are here to express God in thought, word and idea. Our actions must be God-like, we must begin to live the Truth and let our light so shine before men that they will see our good works. "By their fruits ye shall know them."

Are our thoughts Godlike? Millions of people are eunuchs as they live in the world and its problems. They are building treasures on earth where the moth and rust doth consume and thieves break through and steal. We are eunuchs in the sense that because of our fear and foolish beliefs, we lose the capacity to create spiritually. We fail to partake of that mystic or Holy Communion with the Father and shed the radiance of the Light Limitless all around us.

"For there are some eunuchs which were so born from their mother's womb." This means millions follow the old theological pattern of hell and damnation, race mind beliefs, prejudices, and opinions. They are slaves to conditions, traditions and victims of the race thought. They fail to create spiritually and "Come out from among them and be separate." Consequently they are subject to collective or mass thoughts.

"And there are some eunuchs which were made eunuchs of men." We listen to the negative suggestions of others, thereby neutralizing our desire or probability of attainment. A doctor says you will die in six months from heart disease and we accept and believe and prepare to die in six months. We fulfill his verdict "according to our belief is it done unto us."

"And there be eunuchs, which have made themselves eunuchs for the Kingdom of Heaven's sake." This is the man abiding in the pure, illuminated spiritual consciousness. He is constantly in holy communion with the Father within. He wears the seamless robe, the Robe of Glory, the Garment of God which the mystic wears as he moves inward towards the Real. It is the pilgrimage within to the Holy of Holies and no one may enter except he wears the wedding garment. Many are cast out because they have holes, seams and ragged edges in their garments.

When we don white gloves and aprons and appear before the Great White Throne wearing the badge of innocence and purity, the Truth knows us because we know it. Then we inhale the incense always burning there and the precious perfume of His inmost Essence illumines our minds and bodies and we awake whole, complete and perfect. Our healing is instantaneous.

"He that is able to receive it, let him receive it." He that is open minded and receptive enough will realize that this whole drama takes place within himself, in his own consciousness. Such a person then receives or perceives the Truth. Anyone who looks upon this parable as so many rules and regulations laid down by a man called Jesus is wallowing in the mire of the world beliefs and confusion. "He is worshipping the letter of the law." "The letter killeth, the Spirit giveth life."

In prayer, when man contemplates the joy of having or being that which he desires to be or have, he is performing the spiritual marriage act. Man at peace in this state of mental receptivity, may be likened to the wife or womb, for it is this phase of mind which receives impressions. That which man feels himself to be during prayer is the groom, for it is the name or nature he assumes and it therefore leaves its impregnation on his subjective consciousness; so one dies to what he is as one assumes the name and nature of the impregnation. The joy of the answered prayer plus the inner satisfaction that follows the appropriation of man's desire is the proof of his marriage.

# Chapter 12

Let us see these great truths in this new light. The writer has talked to many in various parts of the country who think it is a great sin to dissolve their marriage because the Bible says "What therefore God hath joined together, let not man put asunder." Yet many of these people with whom I have talked live and have lived in hate for many years. This is not a marriage, but a mockery and rank hypocrisy.

Surely common sense dictates that because a man said a few words—"I now pronounce you man and wife"—that such a ceremony was not the meaning of "What therefore God hath joined together, let not man put asunder." This means, instead, man's spiritual convictions, his absolute faith in that for which he prayed. "I and my Father are one." Man, realizing his oneness with the Father within, begins to do the works of God and no power or agency or man can break him asunder from his spiritual knowing or oneness with God.

How often is marriage really a spiritual union? How often is it merely a legal ceremony against which the parties to the contract begin to chafe in a week or so in some cases? Man marries a state of consciousness. A true spiritual union between two people (God hath joined) no one in all the world can put asunder even if he tried his utmost to do so.

To obviate making the wrong choice, man should pray scientifically when desiring a wife. There is no religion without science, and no science without religion. These are two arcs of a circle that meet and become one.

This is the scientific way he should go about selecting a wife. Let him close his eyes, be still and imagine that he is now married to a noble, dignified, loyal, spiritual, wonderful woman. Let him state the qualities or attributes that he admires in a woman and feel that he now is married to such a woman. Then he should go off to sleep knowing that Infinite Intelligence will see to it that he is irresistibly attracted to the right woman.

In such cases he will immediately recognize her and she him. It will be mutual. There will be no confusion. It will be a perfect spiritual union. They will bend spiritually, physically and mentally. Praying in this way, he is not deceived by the evidence of his senses which are nearly always fooling him.

When a man plans to get married, he must never judge according to appearances. Let him "judge righteous judgment." A man came to the author and said the woman he was going with for three years refused to marry him and he was going to commit suicide if he couldn't have her. After being taught to pray scientifically for a wife, this man met a waitress in a hotel where he was staying, fell in love with her and married her. They are supremely happy.

What about the woman that he could not live without? In the interim it was revealed to him through friends that she had already been married six times, never taking the trouble to get a divorce. She was also an ex-convict and had been convicted of several crimes and while keeping company with him was living with another man.

When we pray aright, it does not bring grief or pain to anyone else. Some people think they have the right to break up the homes of others. They say "That's the man I want", and they are perfectly willing to break up the home to gain their point. It is true they may succeed, but what kind of a bargain have they? They have impregnated themselves with limitation and the result is dissatisfaction and unhappiness in many instances.

What has happened to the Golden Rule? Where is it? Have they applied it? "As ye would that men should do unto you, do you even so to them in like manner." This is the whole law of a happy and successful life. In selfishness and greed this is forgotten. What does the woman want the family of the man that she weaned away from his wife to think about her? What does she want them to feel about her? She wants his wife and family to think of her as a noble, gentle, dignified lady who is Christlike. Then let her apply this principle and see if she still desires to wreck their home.

We must stop working in a finite way for an absolute state. Marriages are made in heaven—in other words, harmony and peace. "Peace is the power at the heart of God." God is peace. Jacob, when he prayed for a wife, saw angels ascending and descending. The angels ascending and descending represent the qualities and attributes that man admires in a woman.

"As within, so without." Having felt the reality of the state it becomes subjectified and whatever is subjectively accepted is made manifest. Therefore, he meets the image and likeness of his inner conviction. If man strikes a note on the grand piano, all notes in harmony with it strike in response. They may be higher or lower but similar. So man attracts to himself people based on his moods or concepts of himself. It is affinity or attraction depending on the chord I strike. Man may strike a discord but he does not take all the discords out in order to make a harmony. When he disciplines his mind in prayer, he can play a divine harmony.

Suppose a man "cheats" on his wife. If he had love and respect for his wife, he would not want any other woman. When man has found his true spiritual ideal in marriage, he has no desire for any other woman. Love is a oneness, not a duality or a multiplicity. Man running around with many women—which are but the many adulterous moods within him—is marrying many concepts such as frustration, resentment, cynicism, etc. When man has found love with his mate he has found fullness of life.

The reader may say "Why do some men have many wives?" The reason is that at one time the earth was depopulated and the earthly fathers, not knowing anything better, suggested this method. But today we are more spiritually awakened and know that the earth is populated enough. Therefore, if a man "cheats" on his wife, he is frustrated and never really has had a love or feeling of oneness. He has a profound inferiority complex and is striking that tone. So what is he meeting? He is meeting himself—in other words, his inner mood or concept of himself.

Inevitably, then, the women he meets are vacillating, neurotic women, confused and marrying many concepts. He is but seeing and hearing his own inner vibrations. The women in the case are just as frustrated and unstable as the man. "Birds of a feather flock together." "Like begets like."

Now let us take the case of a woman who is "running around" with a married man. The reason for this is simple to see. She gets a vicarious thrill because she takes him away from his wife—he pours out his troubles and makes disparaging remarks about his wife. She has been unable to demonstrate a husband or boy friend and gets a pseudo-satisfaction, or false thrill in stealing another woman's husband. She too has an inferiority complex and is unstable. She talks of the many proposals she has—it is because she is aching for them.

Now a man who knows the laws of life will always see his wife as he first saw her. In his thought and feeling she will always be clothed with the garment of salvation and the robe of righteousness. Then she will always be to him what he believes her to be. We are not living with people so much as we are living with our concept of them.

If a man never loses faith in his wife, she will fulfill his conception of her. If she becomes dejected, tired and worried and he becomes one with her in feeling, they both fall into the ditch. But if he rejects this mood and knows and feels that she is healed, wonderful and perfect, no matter how despondent or gloomy she may become, he lifts her out of it.

Man demotes himself by feeling his lack. His fear is transmitted to his wife and she reacts in kind.

She cannot see him in the way she formerly did as he has not the same feeling about himself. She can see him only in the way he sees himself. Likewise he can see her only in the way she sees herself.

If a man feels himself to be dignified, he commands respect and gets it. One man having the predominant mood of success and happiness, knits all the members of the household together. He influences them and dominates them mentally. When he dies, quite often the members of the family fight between themselves. He was a cementing influence. He felt harmony and peace in the household. Your dominant conviction makes others see what you see.

"He is not dead—he sleepeth." He realized the Truth and saw life there. He caused the so-called dead man to vibrate. Then they all saw Lazarus alive. "The damsel is not dead, but sleepeth." We are asleep to God. All tones are within us. Men ask, "Should I get a divorce?" This is an individual problem and cannot be generalized. In some cases divorce is not the solution, no more so than marriage is the solution of a lonely man.

Friction between husband and wife can be solved by prayer. Let the wife see the Christ in her husband. Let her see him as he ought to be, happy radiant and peaceful. Let her hear him, in the meditative state, tell her how wonderful she is, how kind she is and how happy he is with her. If she is faithful to this treatment, he will be transformed and peace is restored.

In some cases, of course, there never was a real marriage. Because a man and woman have a marriage license and live in a home, it does not follow that that is a real home. Perhaps it is a place of discord and hate. When a child is present and the parents do not know the law of life, it is better to break up such a union than have the mood of hate stifle the minds of the children. Many times a child's life and mind are dwarfed by the mood of the parents, resulting in neurosis, crime, etc. It is far better for a boy to live with one parent who loves him, than to live with two who hate each other and fight all the time.

Divorce may be right for one person and wrong for another. "There is now no condemnation of them that are in Christ Jesus." Where there is no consciousness of guilt, there is no guilt. A divorced woman may be far more noble and Christ-like than many of her married sisters who are living a lie, rather than face the Truth. Such a married life is a sham and a farce though they manage to keep up appearances. They are afraid of what the neighbors will say. Others are afraid that it would be bad for John's business. Others stay married for political reasons, etc.

This, of course, is making a mockery of marriage. Marriage on the physical plane is symbolic of the spiritual, esoteric union of two souls seeking their way back to the heart of Reality which is Love. God is love.

To say that a divorced person is under divine condemnation is a mockery and a sham and shows a complete lack of understanding. In many cases it is the decent, honorable thing to do. In some cases where a couple find they are hopelessly incompatible, spiritually and mentally, then let them do as a friend of the author's did recently. He said to his wife, "Goodbye and God bless you." She replied, "Goodby and God bless you, Harry." They both meant it. They were blessed and there is absolutely no guilt because they have no consciousness of guilt.

Man forgives himself. There is no one else to forgive him. "Hath no man condemned thee? Neither do I condemn thee." We can divorce each other and yet love one another. Love is the fulfillment of the law. Love is an impersonal law. The love spoken of is the impersonal good will, rejoicing that the law of God or good is working for the other and through him that the peace of God is in his home, heart and affairs. Anyone can do this. This is God's love. Love gives— it frees—it is the Spirit of God. Love is the key that opens the treasures of heaven.

True marriage finds its bliss, its happiness in an accord of ideals, a harmony and purity of purpose. Let us stop blaming God for the abuses that go on under the name of marriage. The name to many means sounding brass and tinkling cymbal—a mockery of the word. Let us awake and discover the true impersonal and universal love, then marriage will be a happy state or union, blessed by the fire of Divine Love.

Love seeketh not her own. Love is and all there is, is Love. Love is the knot that binds man and woman (thought and feeling) in the endless cord of life, binding past and future in the eternal present. All that was, and all that shall be now is, for in Love's eyes time is not. Love is the end of the quest and the goal thereof and Love is the way of life. Take heed that ye despise not God in human form. He may be at your side in the person of your beloved one, through the working of God's grace. The desire for freedom is oftentimes a desire to marry another. A lady gets a divorce, for example, and she is bitter and resentful towards her former husband. She remarries without forgiving and what does she find? The second is worse than the first. She tries a third and a fourth and a fifth. Each is worse than the preceding one. All the while she does not know that her inner mood of resentment caused her to attract similar types of men based upon the laws of attraction.

The cure is to give herself a mood of love and peace for the mood of resentment, then she has forgiven (given for) herself. She has given the mood of love for the mood of hate and is at peace. Living in the mood of resentment over supposed wrongs committed by a former husband caused her to attract lack and limitation because she was living and moving in the attitude of lack.

Her ideas of love and marriage have to change if she seeks to find true harmony. She must lift love to a spiritual basis. Let's not limit love, bind it or circumscribe it. Love, freedom, and respect, these three are one and the one is three. If any of them is absent, there is no love present. The three are synonymous.

The contemplation of divine ideals—the study of the mysteries of life—a common purpose and plan and personal freedom bring about that mystic marriage, the wedded bliss, that holy union where the two souls become one. Each is wedded to God. Let us remember who we are—sons of God on a journey of self discovery.

The journey we take is the pilgrimage within to the Holy of Holies and the God we seek is the subliminal essence or the perfumed presence of our own I AMness. "Had I not come they would not have known sin." Our sin is our failure to realize our desire and live a full and happy life. To live the life, let us sing the Song of the Lamb. I am Christ is the song. Feel it. Believe it. Act it! For its word must become flesh!

The esoteric meaning of "the grand passion" is true marriage. The inner meaning of sex on its psycho-mystical side may be, in a manner, described as a craving for subconscious respiration of loftier levels of Reality. The divine alchemy of the grand passion functions through and beyond its mechanisms and rituals and makes possible the approach and experience of the Beloved One.

Katherine Mansfield in her journal says, "A sudden idea of the relationship between lovers—We are neither male or female, we are a compound of both. I choose the male who will develop and expand the male in me; he chooses me to expand the female in him. Being made "whole"—By love serve ye one another." Jesus in the New Sayings is reported to have answered the query as to when the Kingdom of Heaven will come by the words, "When there shall no longer be male or female" (in a divided undisciplined state of consciousness).

In the gospel of the Holy Twelve Jesus says, "Verily I say unto you, In God there is neither male, nor female and yet both are one, and God is the Two in One. He is She and She is He. The Elohim our God, is Perfect, Infinite and One."

# About the Author

A native of Ireland who resettled in America, Joseph Murphy, Ph.D., D.D. (1898–1981) was a prolific and widely admired New Thought minister and writer, best known for his metaphysical classic, *The Power of Your Subconscious Mind*, an international bestseller since it first appeared on the self-help scene in 1963. A popular speaker, Murphy lectured on both American coasts and in Europe, Asia, and South Africa. His many books and pamphlets on the auto-suggestive and metaphysical faculties of the human mind have entered multiple editions—some of the most poignant of which appear in this volume. Murphy is considered one of the pioneering voices of affirmative-thinking philosophy.

Printed in the USA
CPSIA information can be obtained
at www.ICGtesting.com
JSHW061935240124
55991JS00004B/155

9 781722 501310